**HEINEMANN LIBRARY**

# Foundation Maths
# Dictionary

www.heinemann.co.uk/library
Visit our website to find out more information about Heinemann Library books.
To order:
 Phone 44 (0) 1865 888066
 Send a fax to 44 (0) 1865 314091
 Visit the Heinemann Bookshop at www.heinemann.co.uk/library to browse our catalogue and order online.

First published in Great Britain by Heinemann Library, Halley Court, Jordan Hill, Oxford OX2 8EJ, a division of Reed Educational and Professional Publishing Ltd.
Heinemann is a registered trademark of Reed Educational and Professional Publishing Ltd.

OXFORD MELBOURNE AUCKLAND
JOHANNESBURG BLANTYRE GABORONE
IBADAN PORTSMOUTH (NH) USA CHICAGO

© David Kirkby 2001
The moral right of the author has been asserted.

All rights reserved. No part of this publication may be reproduced, stored in a retrieval system, or transmitted in any form or by any means, electronic, mechanical, photocopying, recording, or otherwise, without either the prior written permission of the publishers or a licence permitting restricted copying in the United Kingdom issued by the Copyright Licensing Agency Ltd, 90 Tottenham Court Road, London W1P 0LP.

Designed by Jonathan Williams
Illustrated by Simone Abel, Oxford Illustrators and Jonathan Williams
Originated by Ambassador Litho Ltd
Printed and bound by Edelvives, Zaragoza

ISBN 0 431 01311 X
05 04 03 02 01
10 9 8 7 6 5 4 3 2 1

British Library Cataloguing in Publication Data

Kirkby, David
Heinemann Library Foundation maths dictionary
1. Mathematics – Dictionaries, Juvenile
I. Title II. Maths Dictionary
51C.3

## array

**Arrays** are made from **rows** and **columns**.

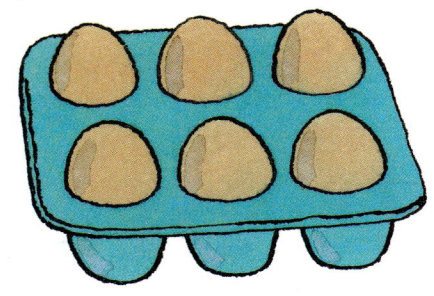

2 rows and 3 columns.　　　　3 rows and 5 columns.

## balance

When two things **weigh** the same amount they **balance**.

## block graph   See also: graph

A **block graph** shows information about amounts of things using blocks.

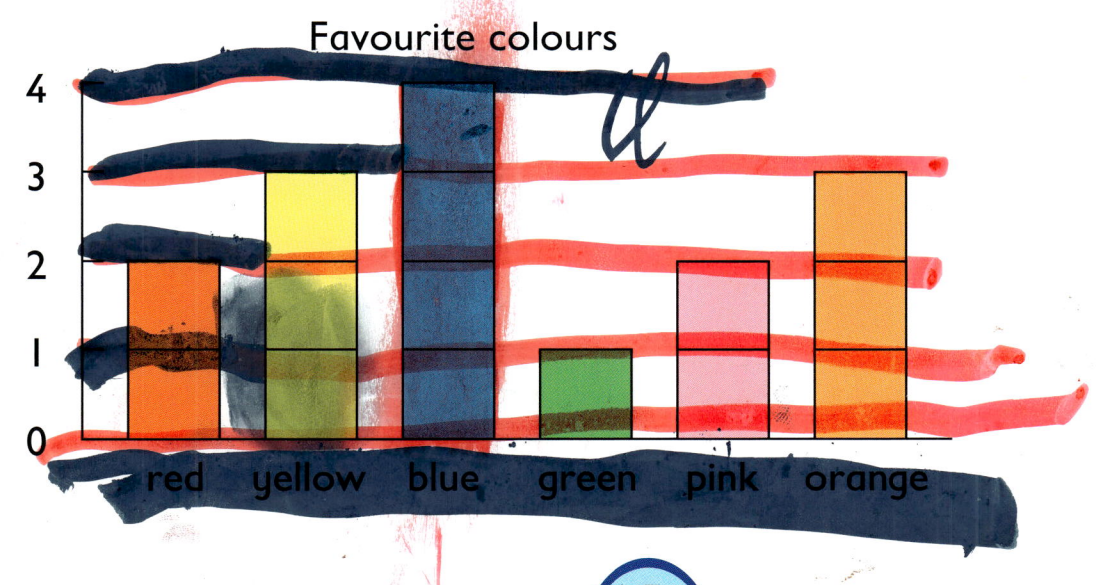

5

## calculate, calculation
See also: operation, mental

You **calculate** when you work out something.

These are **calculations**.

## capacity
**Capacity** is the amount a container will hold. You **measure** capacity in **litres** and **millilitres**.

The capacity of this bottle is 1 litre (1l).

## centimetre

A **centimetre** is a **measure** of **length**.

The marks on this ruler are one centimetre apart.
The finger is 5 centimetres **long**.

**cm** is short for centimetre.
100 centimetres is a **metre**.

1 cm

## centre

The **centre** is the middle point of a shape or object.

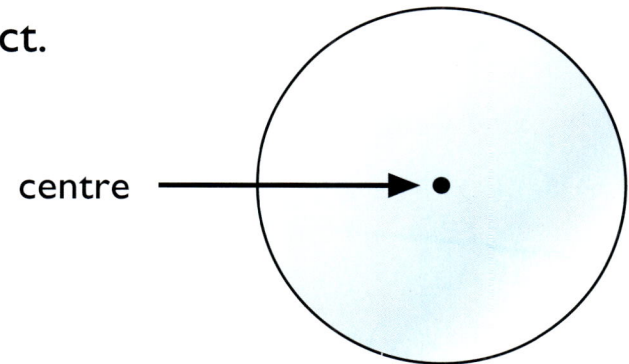

## change

You get **change** when you pay for an object with a **coin** of a higher value.

## circle, circular

A **circle** is a perfectly round shape.
It has one **curved** **side**.

These stickers are **circular**. They are circle shaped.

## clockwise    See also: anti-clockwise

The hands of a clock move in a **clockwise** direction.

 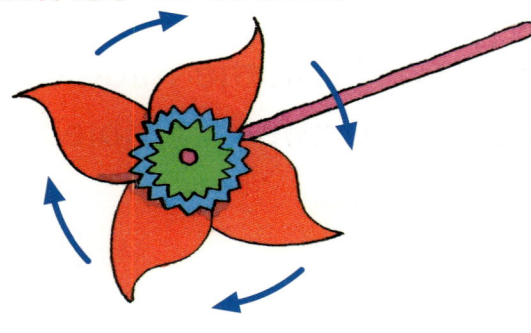

## coin

**Coins** are money.
Coins are worth 1p, 2p, 5p, 10p, 20p, 50p, £1 or £2.

## column   See also: array

A **column** is a line of objects or **numbers**, one above the other.

Five columns of bricks.

| Zac | Sal | Jan | Amy |
|-----|-----|-----|-----|
| 4 | 3 | 2 | 1 |
| 1 | 4 | 0 | 3 |
| 2 | 1 | 3 | 4 |
| 3 | 2 | 0 | 1 |
| 5 | 0 | 4 | 2 |

A chart with four columns.

## cone

A **cone** is a solid shape with one pointed end and one **circular** end.

## corner

A **corner** is where the **sides** or **edges** of a shape meet.

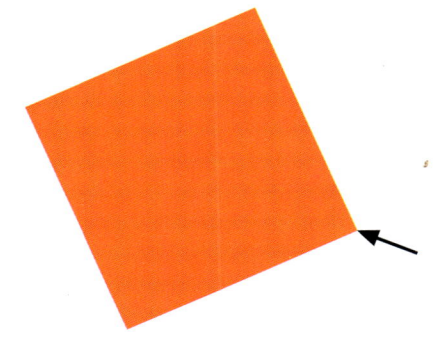

corners

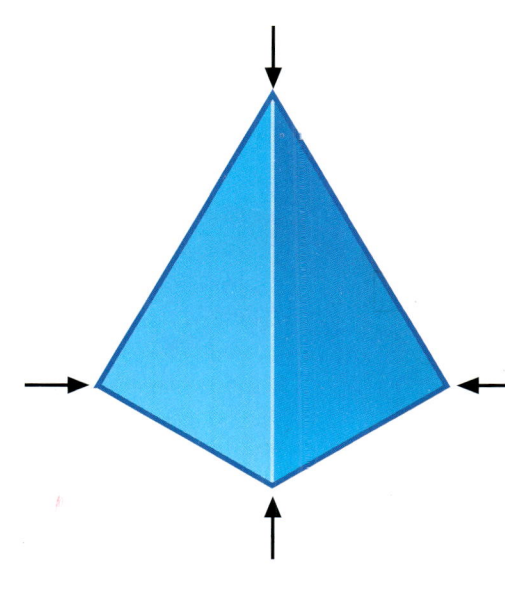

## cube

A **cube** is a **solid** shape.
Cubes have 6 **square faces**.
All the faces are the same size.

## cuboid

A **cuboid** is a solid shape with 6 **rectangular faces**.
Most boxes are cuboids.

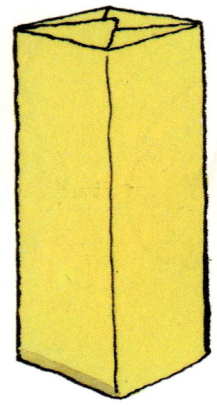
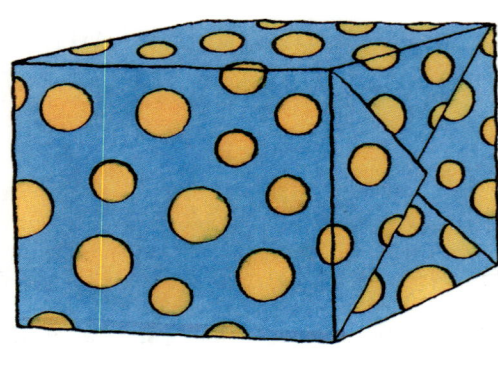

## curved

A **curved** line is not **straight**.
These lines are curved.

## cylinder

A **cylinder** is a **solid** shape with a **circular face** at each end and a **curved** face between.

## day   See also: month, tomorrow, yesterday

A **day** is 24 **hours** long.
There are seven days in a **week**.

## difference

The **difference** between two **numbers** is how much **more** or **less** one is than the other.

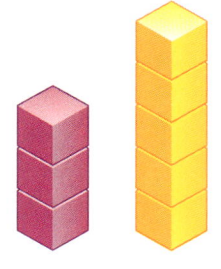

The difference between 3 and 5 is 2.

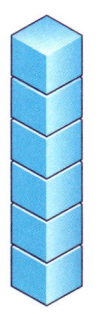

The difference between 6 and 2 is 4.

## digit

**See also: digital clock, place value, three-digit number, two-digit number**

A **digit** is one of the counting **numbers**:
0, 1, 2, 3, 4, 5, 6, 7, 8, 9.

These are digit cards.

## digital clock

A **digital clock** uses **digits** to show the time.

**divide, divided by, division**   See also: operation

You **divide** when you share or group things into equal **sets**.

÷ This sign means **'divided by'**.

The 8 biscuits have been divided by 2. They are shared into 2 groups with 4 biscuits in each.

**8 ÷ 2 = 4**

The 12 buns have been divided into groups of 4. There are 3 groups with 4 buns in each.

**12 ÷ 4 = 3**

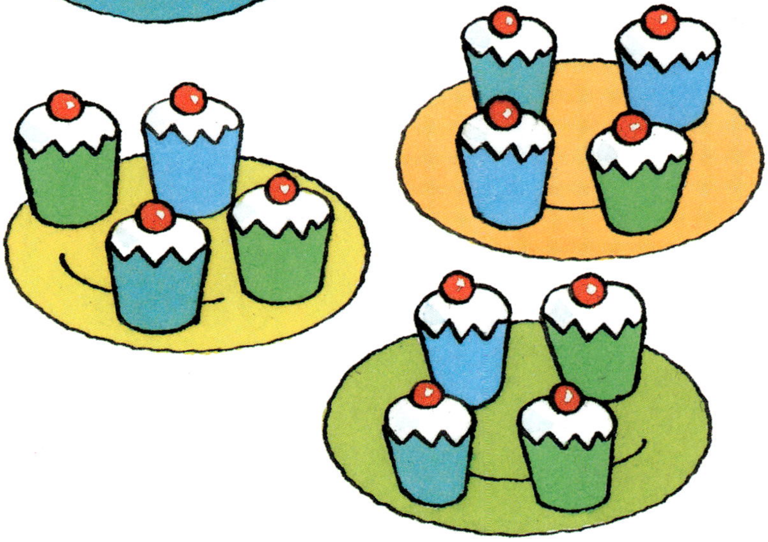

**Division** is the opposite of **multiplication**.

**double**

**Double** a **number** is two times the number, or **twice** the number.

Double 4 is 8.          Double 6 is 12.

## edge

Solid shapes have edges where two faces meet.

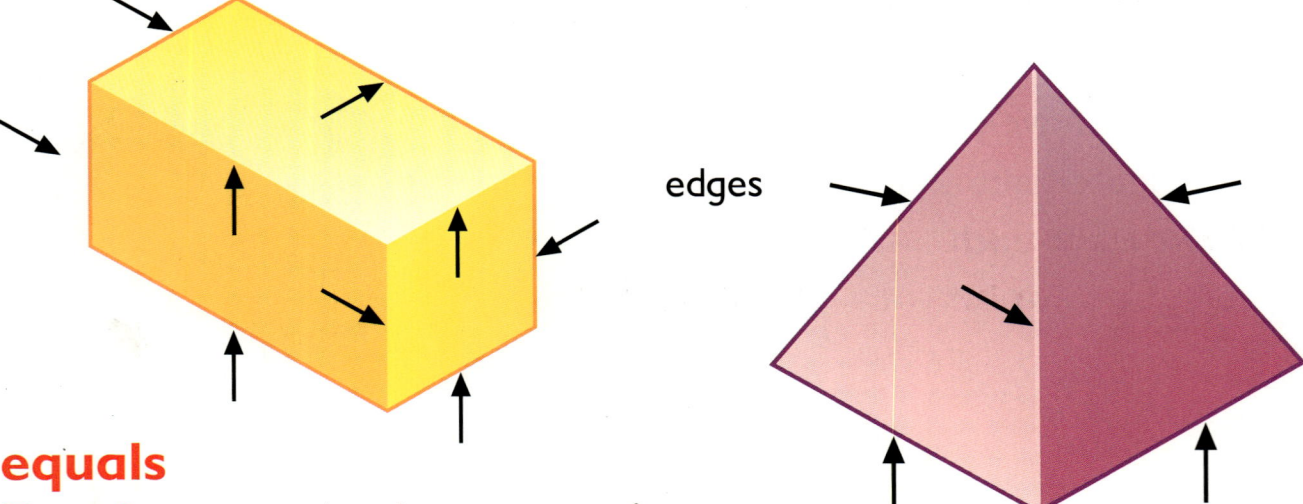

## equals

Equals means 'is the same as'.

= This is an equals sign.

## estimate

An estimate is a good guess to decide how much.

How long? About 5 centimetres.

How much? About £1.     How many? About 70.

**even number**
An **even number** can be **divided** exactly by two.

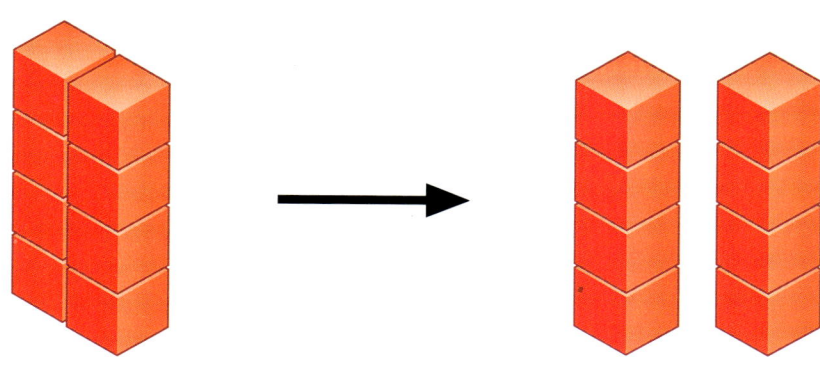

These are even numbers.
The missing numbers are **odd numbers**.

**face**
Solid shapes have **faces**.
They can be **flat** or **curved**.

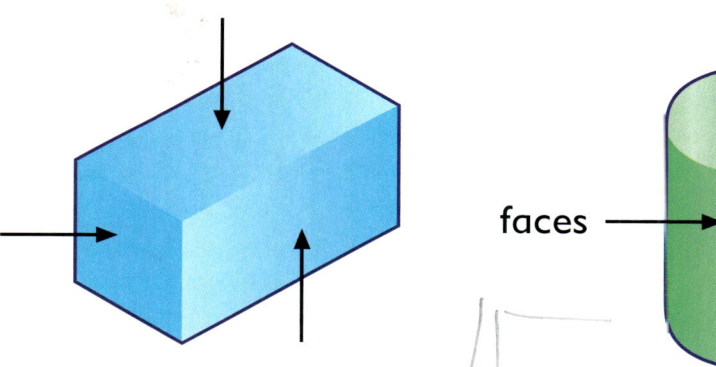

faces

**few, fewer, fewest**
**Few** means small in **number**, not many.

Pip has **fewer** spots than Ross.
Ross has fewer spots than Sam.
Pip has **fewest** spots.

15

**flat**   See also: corner, side

These are **flat** shapes. They have **length** and width but no thickness.

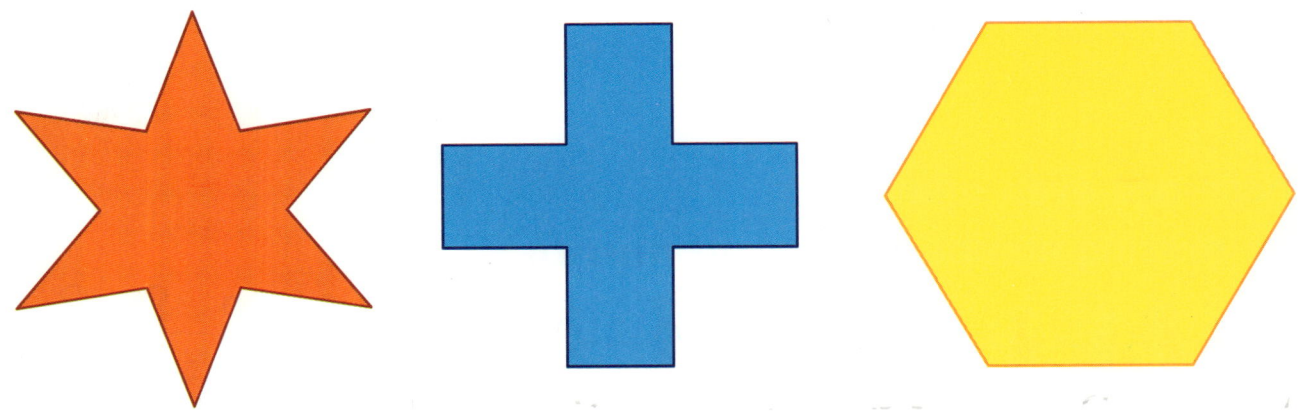

**fortnight**

A **fortnight** is 2 **weeks** or 14 **days**.

A fortnight to go!

**fraction**

A **fraction** is part of a whole one.

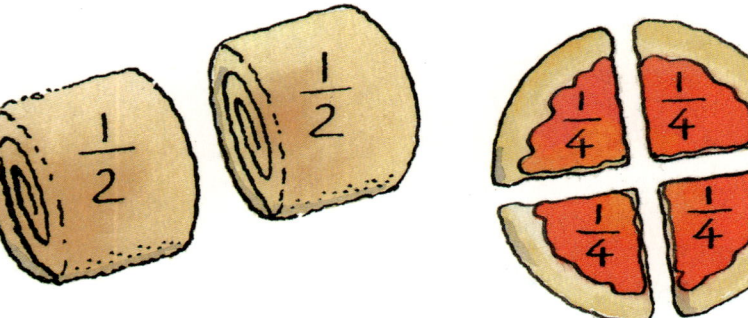

Each piece is a fraction of the whole one.

## gram

A **gram** is a **measure** of **weight**.

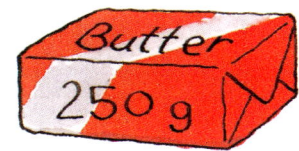

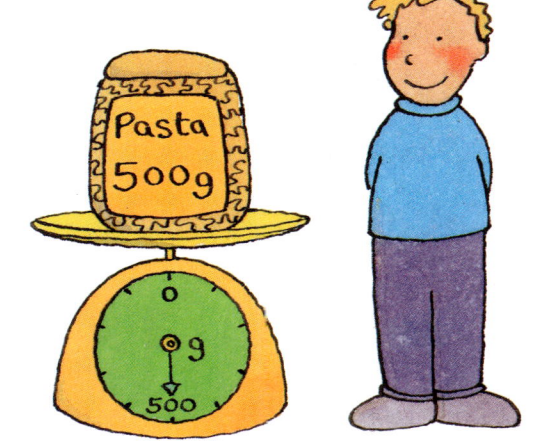

**g** is short for gram.
1000 grams is a **kilogram**.

## graph

See also: pictogram, block graph

A **graph** is a chart that shows information about amounts of things.

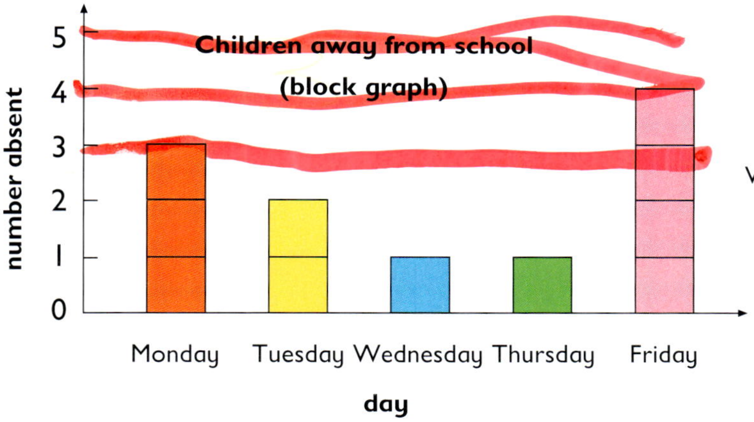

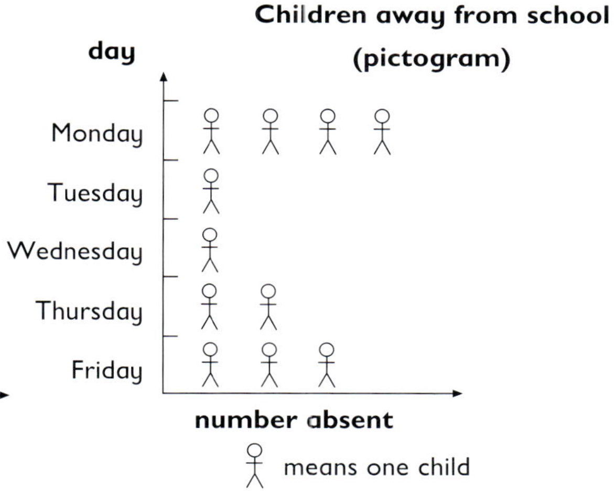

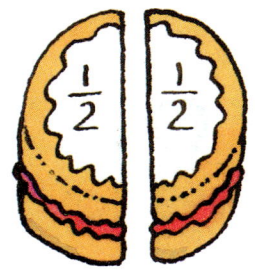

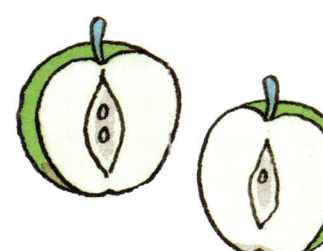

## half, halve

See also: half past, half turn

Each of these is a **half**.
A half is a **fraction**.
There are two halves in a whole.

When you **halve** something, you **divide** it into two equal parts.

a b c d e f g h i j k l m n o p q r s t u v w x y z

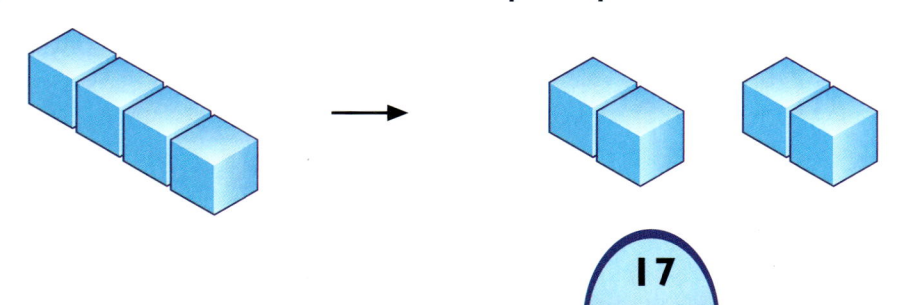

## half past

**Half past** means half way between two 'o'clock' times.
It is 30 minutes past the hour.

half past two

## half turn

A **half turn** is a half of a **whole turn**.
Two half turns make one whole turn.

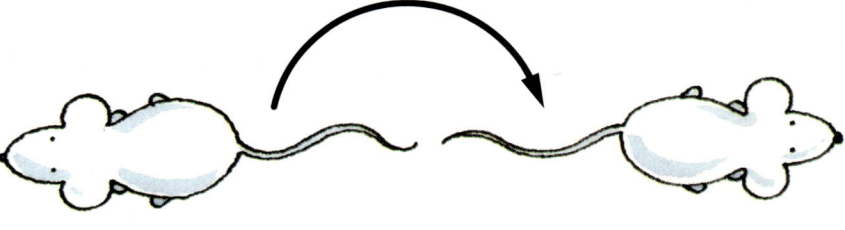

## heavy, heavier, heaviest

**Heavy** means having a lot of **weight**.

The bear is **heavier** than the adult.
The adult is heavier than the child.
The bear is the **heaviest**.

# hexagon
A **hexagon** has 6 **straight sides** and 6 **corners**.

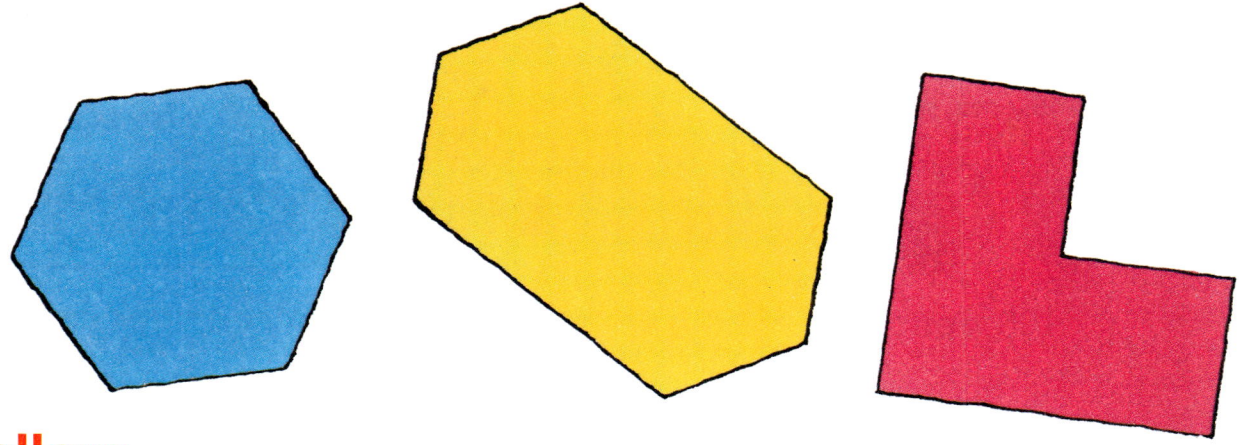

# hollow
These shapes are **hollow**.
They have space inside. They are not **solid**.

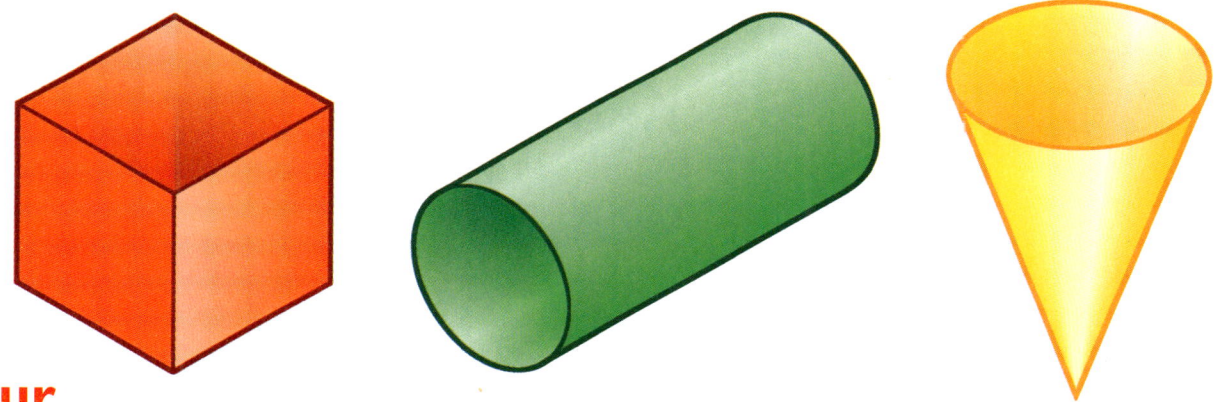

# hour
An **hour** is a **measure** of time. An hour is 60 **minutes** long.
There are 24 hours in a **day**.

## hundred, hundred square

Ten lots of ten make one **hundred**.

100 pence

One **hundred square**.

## kilogram

A **kilogram** is a **measure** of **weight**.

**kg** is short for kilogram.
A kilogram is 1000 **grams**.

## length

The **length** of a line or object is the distance from one end to the other.

6cm

The length an event can also be measured.

1 hour

12:00 → 1:00

lunchtime starts

lunchtime ends

## less, least
**Less** or **least** is the smaller or smallest **number** or amount.

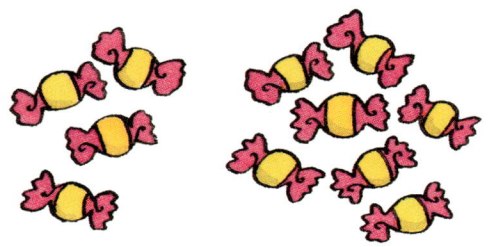

4 is less than 7.          The spoon **weighs** less than the bowl.

John has saved less than Sarah.
Syeda has saved less than John.
Syeda has saved the least.

## light, lighter, lightest
**Light** means having little **weight**.

A feather is light.

The cat is **lighter** than the dog.
The rabbit is lighter than the cat.
The rabbit is the **lightest**.

## line

A **line** is drawn from one point to another.
It has length but no width. It can be **straight** or **curved**.

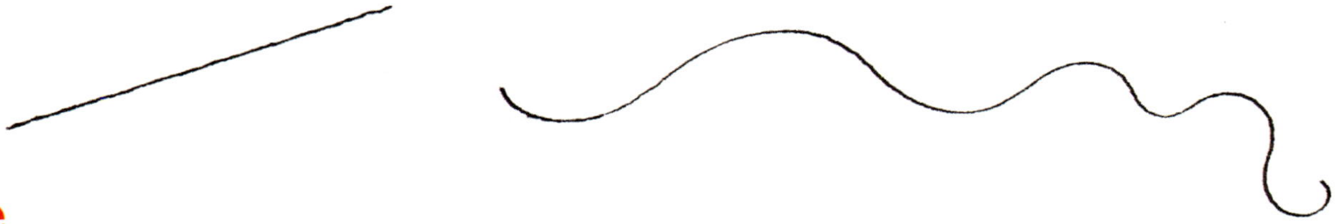

## litre

You use **litres** to **measure** amounts of liquids.
A litre is a measure of **capacity**.

**l** is short for litre.
A litre is 1000 **millilitres**.

## long, longer, longest   See also: metre

**Long, longer, longest** describe **length**.

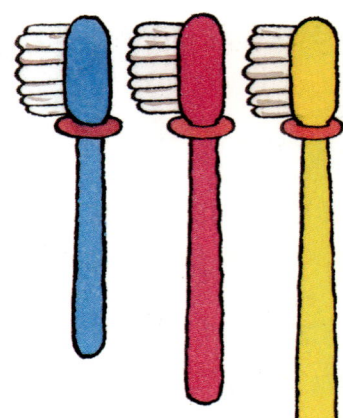

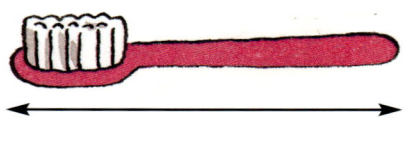

12 centimetres

The pink toothbrush is 12 **centimetres long**.
The pink toothbrush is **longer** than the blue toothbrush.
The yellow toothbrush is the **longest**.

## measure, measuring scale

You **measure** things to find out their size.
**Length**, **weight**, **capacity** and time are different kinds of measure.

measuring scale

## mental

**Mental** means 'in your head'.
You do mental **calculations** in your head.

## metre, metre stick

A **metre** is a **measure** of **length**.
A metre is 100 **centimetres**.

**m** is short for metre.

**Metre sticks** help you measure how **long** things are.
The giraffe is 5 metres **tall**.

1m = 100 cm

## midday
**Midday** is 12 o'clock in the daytime.
It is the end of the morning, and the start of the afternoon.

## midnight
**Midnight** is 12 o'clock at night.
It is the end of one **day,**
and the start of the next.

## millilitre
You use **millilitres** to **measure** amounts of liquids.
A millilitre is a measure of **capacity**.

**ml** is short for millilitre.
1000 millilitres is a **litre**.

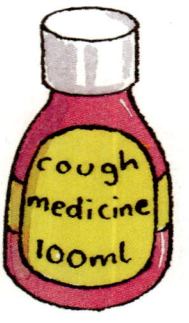 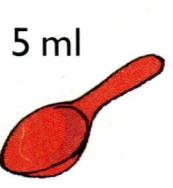  

5 ml

## minus

− This is a **minus** sign.
It means '**subtract**' or 'take away'.

Six minus four **equals** two.

## minute

A **minute** is a short **measure** of time.
A minute is 60 **seconds**.
There are 60 minutes in an **hour**.

## month

There are 12 **months** in a **year**.
There are 28, 29, 30 or 31 **days** in a month.

January 31
February 28/29
March 31
April 30
May 31
June 30
July 31
August 31
September 30
October 31
November 30
December 31

25

## more, most
More or most is the greater or greatest number or amount.

5 is more than 3.

There are more oranges than apples.

Kim has most tomatoes.
Ravi has most eggs.
John has most chips.

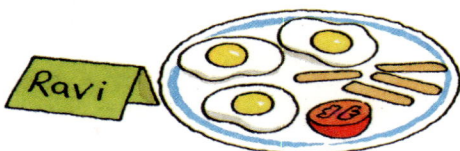

## multiple
When you multiply two numbers together, the answer is a multiple.

| 1 x 2 = 2 | 1 x 5 = 5 |
| 2 x 2 = 4 | 2 x 5 = 10 |
| 3 x 2 = 6 | 3 x 5 = 15 |
| 4 x 2 = 8 | 4 x 5 = 20 |
| 5 x 2 = 10 | 5 x 5 = 25 |
| 6 x 2 = 12 | 6 x 5 = 30 |
| 7 x 2 = 14 | 7 x 5 = 35 |
| 8 x 2 = 16 | 8 x 5 = 40 |
| 9 x 2 = 18 | 9 x 5 = 45 |
| 10 x 2 = 20 | 10 x 5 = 50 |

**The multiples of 2.**   **The multiples of 5.**

## multiply, multiplied by, multiplication

**See also: operation**

You **multiply** when you find how many things there are in a number of same-size groups.

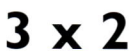

**X** This is a **multiplication** sign.
It means 'times', 'lots of' or '**multiplied by**'.

Three lots of two.
Three times two.
Three twos.

**3 x 2**

Five lots of three.
Five times three.
Five threes.

**5 x 3**

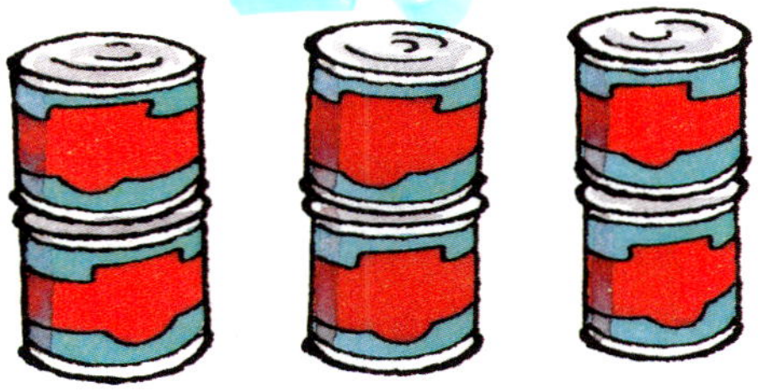

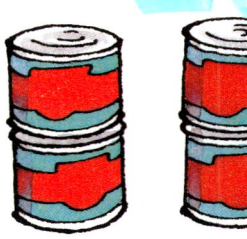

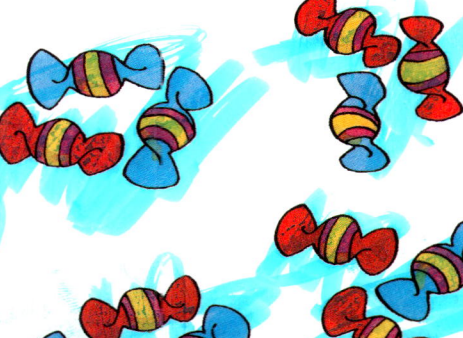

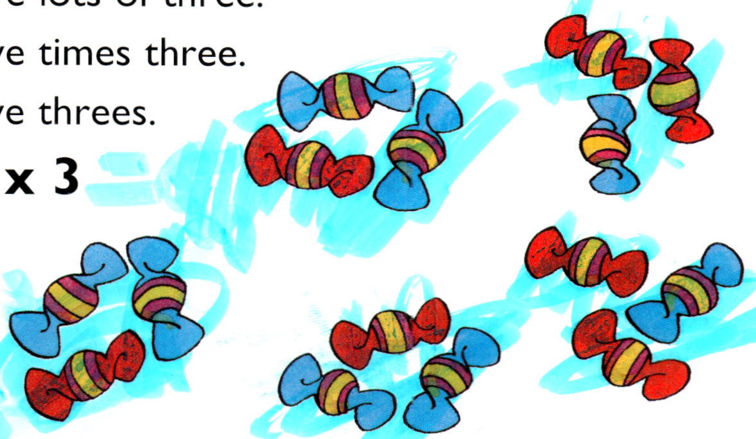

Multiplication is the opposite of **division**.

## nought

**Nought** means nothing or **zero**.
It is written as a **0**

## number, numeral

**Numbers** are used for counting.
They tell you how many there are of something.
Numbers can be written as **numerals**.

a b c d e f g h i j k l m n o p q r s t u v w x y z

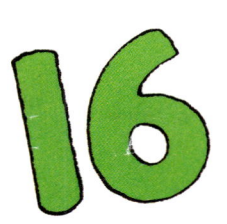

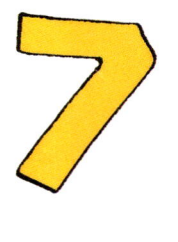

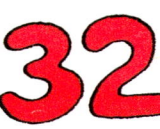

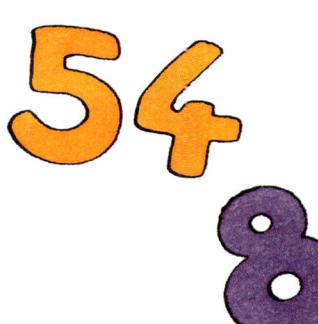

## penny, pence

A **penny** is a small amount of money. Pennies are often called **pence**.

**1p** is short for one penny or one pence. There are 100 pennies in a **pound**.

1p **coins**

## pentagon

A **pentagon** has 5 **straight sides** and 5 **corners**.

## pictogram

A **pictogram** shows information using pictures or symbols. Each picture or symbol stands for an amount. This is shown in a key.

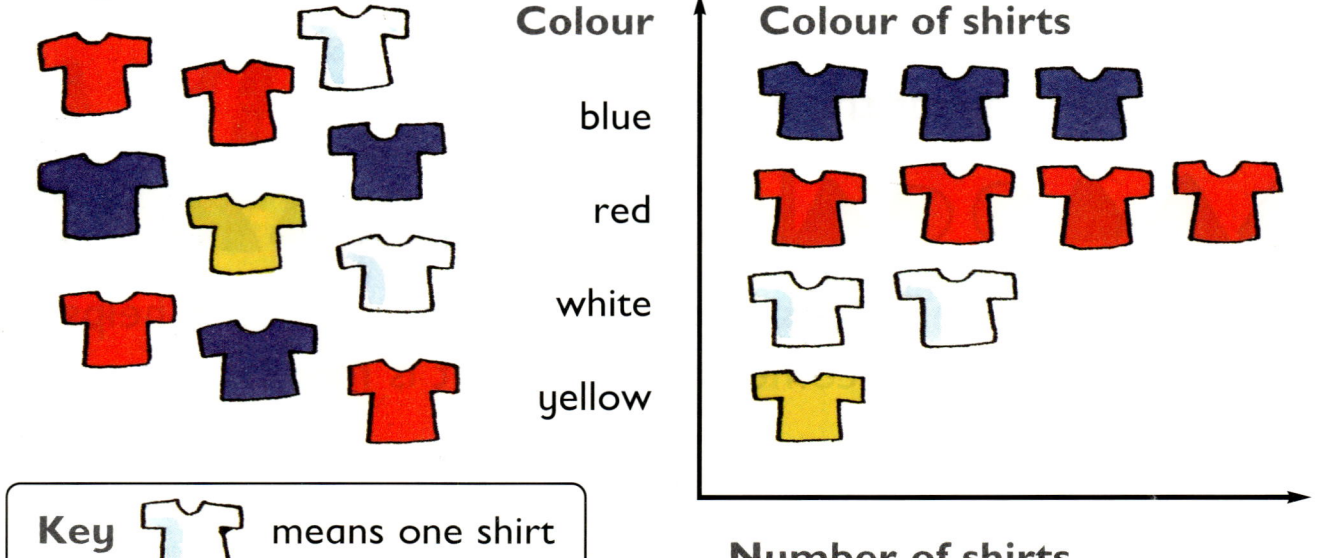

Key  means one shirt

## place value

The **place value** of a **digit** is how much it is worth.

In the number **361**

the digit 3 means 3 hundreds

the digit 6 means 6 tens

the digit 1 means 1 unit.

| H | T | U |
|---|---|---|
| 3 | 6 | 1 |

## plus

**+** This is a **plus** sign.
It means '**add**'.

Two plus five **equals** seven.

Six plus four equals ten.

## point

A **point** marks a place or position.

This arrow shows the point where 9 would be.

0             number line           10

## pound

A **pound** is an amount of money.
One pound is 100 **pennies** or **pence**.

**£6** is short for six pounds.

£1 coins

## price

The **price** of an object is how much money it costs.

Price 30p   Price 25p

## pyramid

A **pyramid** is a **solid** shape. The bottom of a pyramid can be any shape with **straight sides**. The other **faces** are **triangles** and meet at a **point**.

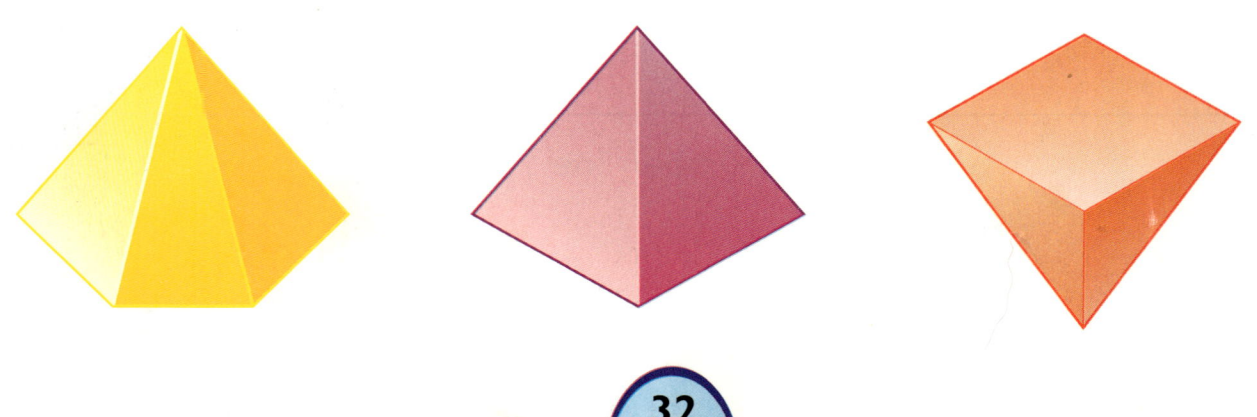

## quarter
See also: quarter past, quarter to, quarter turn

A **quarter** is a **fraction**. There are four quarters in a whole.

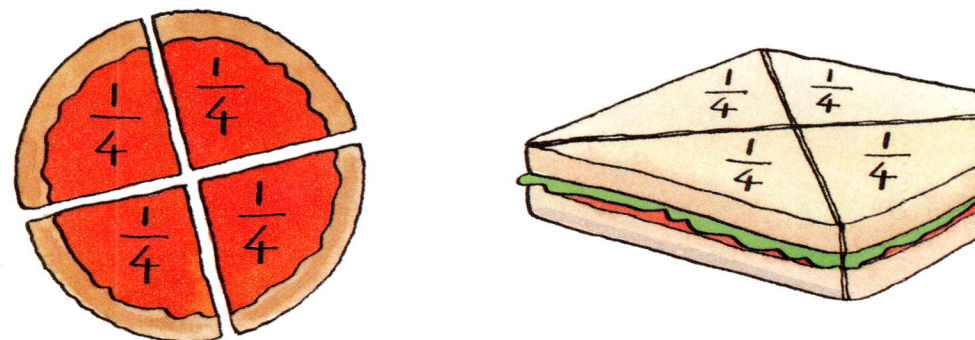

If you **divide** something into four equal parts, each part is a quarter.

A quarter of 8 is 2.

## quarter past
A **quarter** of the **hour** has past.
It is 15 **minutes** past the hour.

quarter past one

## quarter to
There is a **quarter** of an **hour** until the next 'o'clock'.
It is 45 **minutes** past the hour.

quarter to five

## quarter turn

A **quarter turn** is a **quarter** of a **whole turn**.
One quarter turn is a **right angle**.
Four quarter turns make one whole turn.

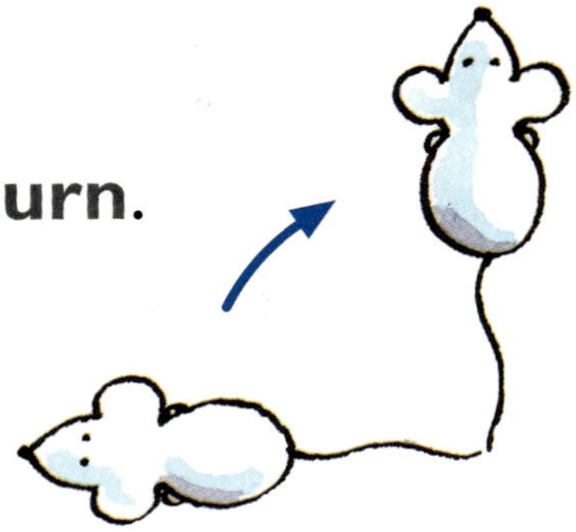

## rectangle, rectangular

A **rectangle** has 4 straight **sides** and 4 **corners**.
It has a **right angle** at each corner.

These paintings are **rectangular**.
They are rectangle shaped.

## reflection

A **reflection** is what you see in a mirror.
One side of a **symmetrical** shape is a reflection of the other.

 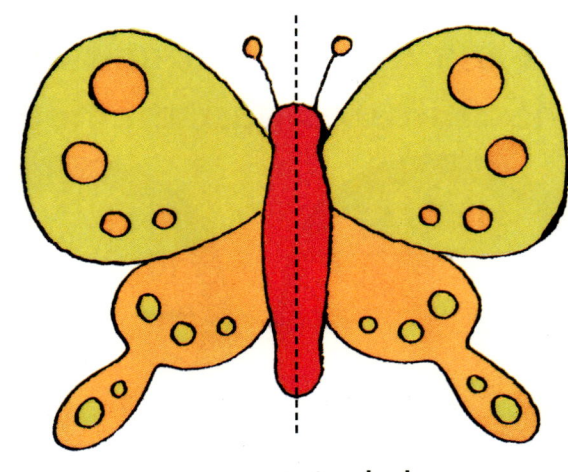

a symmetrical shape

## right angle

A **right angle** is one **quarter turn**.
Each **corner** of a **rectangle** is a right angle.

## round   See also: estimate

You can **round** a **number** to its nearest **multiple** of 10, or 100.

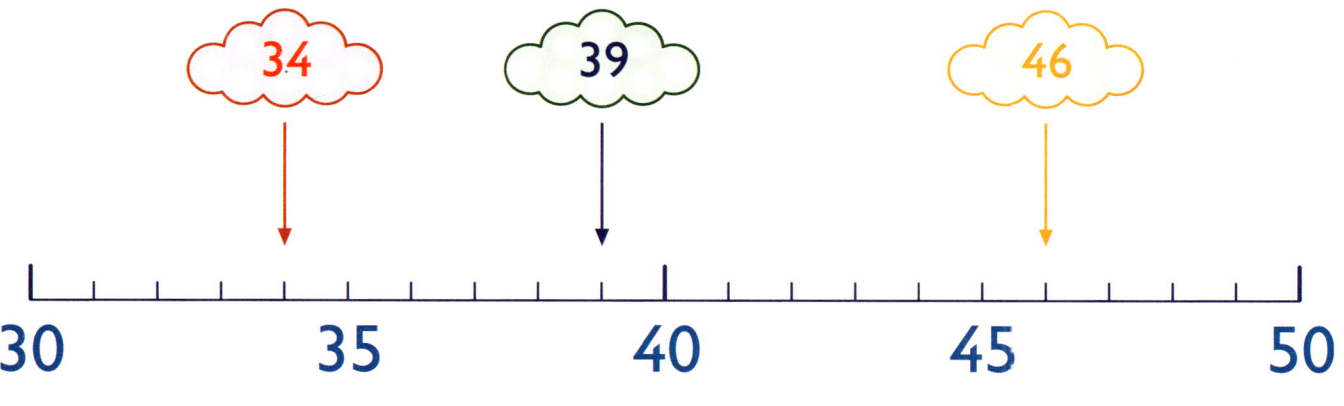

34 rounds down to 30.    39 rounds up to 40.    46 rounds up to 50.

## row   See also: array

A **row** is a line of objects or **numbers**, side by side.

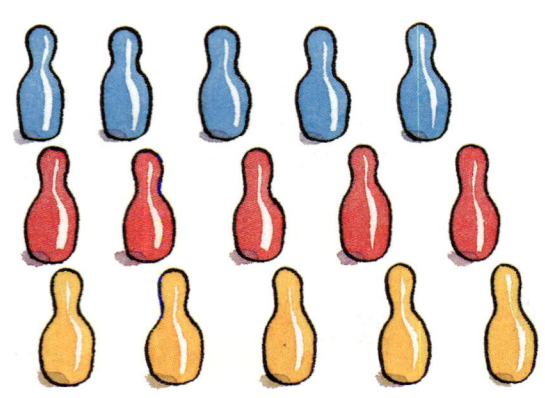
3 rows of skittles.

4 rows of stamps.

## ruler

A **ruler** is a **straight edge** with a **measuring scale** marked on it.
You can use a ruler to draw a straight **line**.

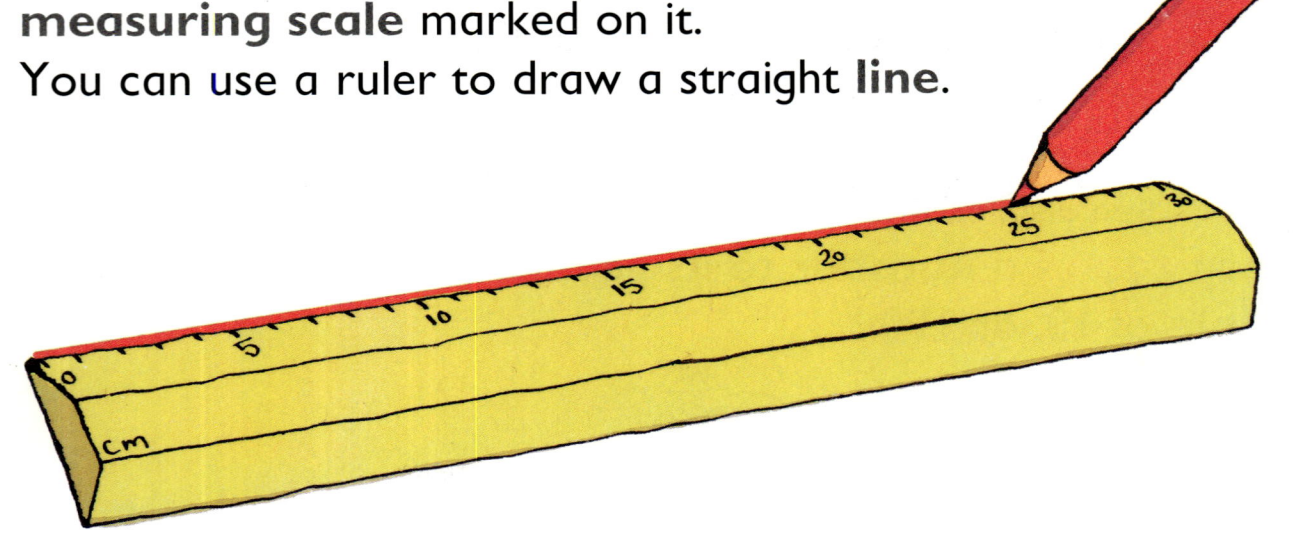

You can use a ruler to **measure length**.

## season

**Seasons** name the time of the **year**.
There are 4 seasons.

spring     summer     autumn     winter

## second

A **second** is a very short **measure** of time.
There are 60 seconds in a **minute**.

Some watches have a hand that counts the seconds.

## sequence
A **sequence** is a **set** of **numbers** or shapes with a **pattern**.

| 1 | 3 | 5 | 7 | 9 | 11 |
|---|---|---|---|---|---|
| 2 | 4 | 6 | 8 | 10 | 12 |
| 5 | 10 | 15 | 20 | 25 | 30 |

△ ■ ⬟ ⬢ ⬣ ...

## set
A **set** is a group of **numbers**, shapes or objects that are alike in some way.

The set of even numbers from 1 to 10

Set of triangles

## short, shorter, shortest
**Short, shorter, shortest** describe **length**.

The white straw and the green straw are short.
The pink straw is shorter than the blue straw.
The green straw is the shortest.

**side**  See also: corner

**Flat** shapes have **sides**.
Sides can be **straight** or **curved**.

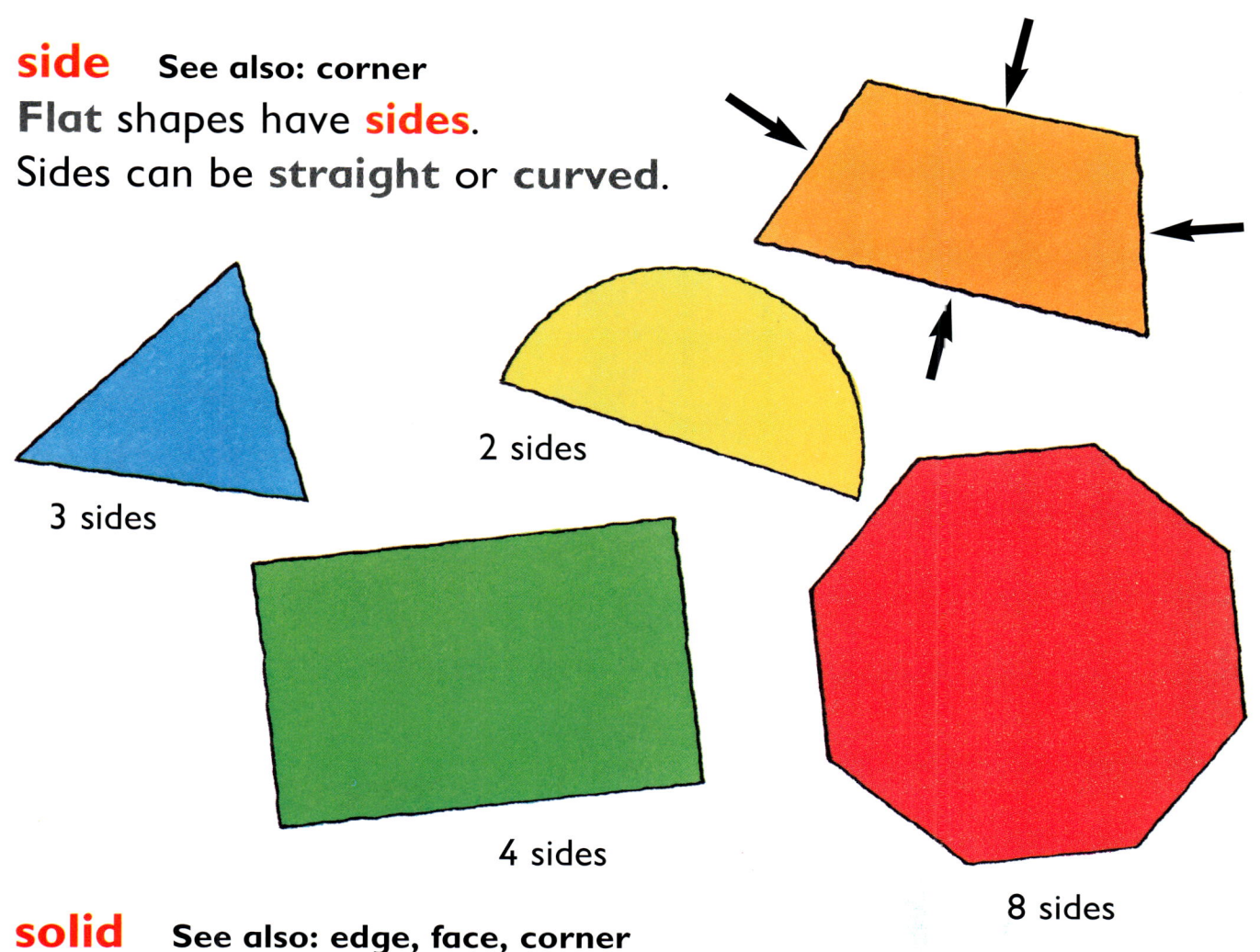

2 sides

3 sides

4 sides

8 sides

**solid**  See also: edge, face, corner

These are **solid** shapes.
There is no space inside.

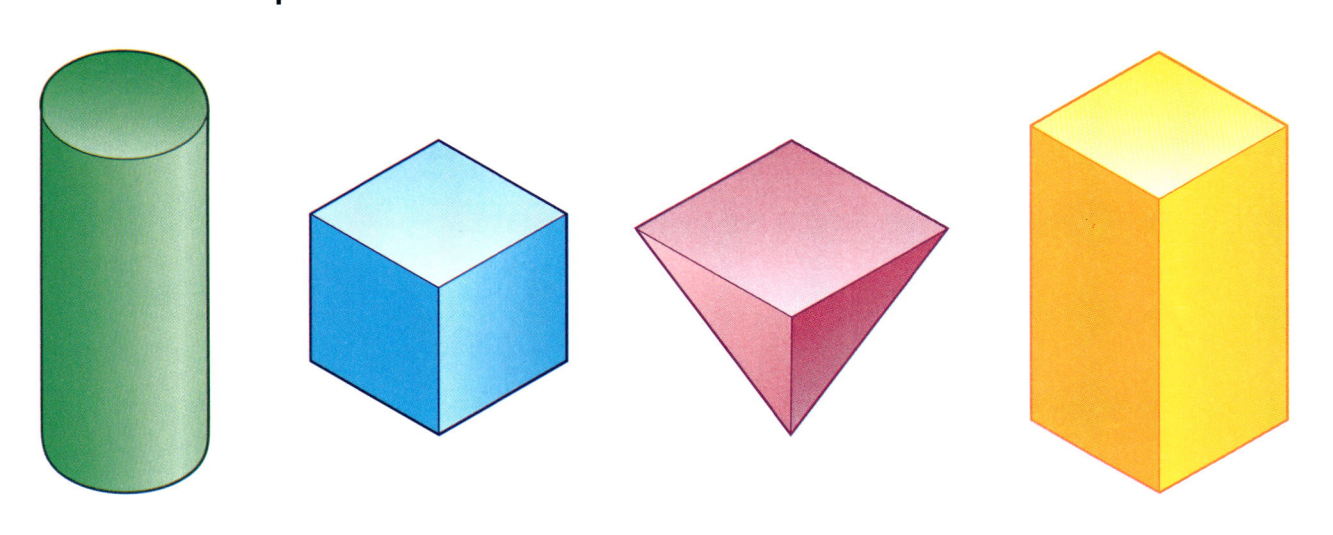

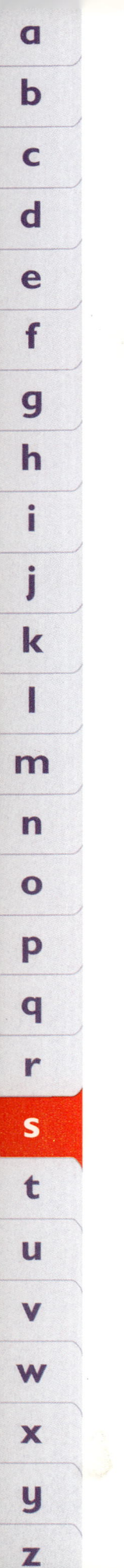

## sphere
A **sphere** is perfectly round, like a ball.

## square    See also: rectangle
A **square** has 4 **straight sides** and 4 **corners**.
All the sides are the same **length**.
All the corners are **right angles**.

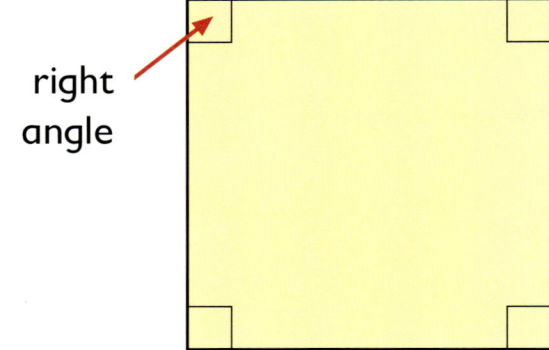

right angle

## star
A star is a **flat** shape with several points.

A five-pointed star.                A six-pointed star.

## straight

These **lines** are all **straight**.

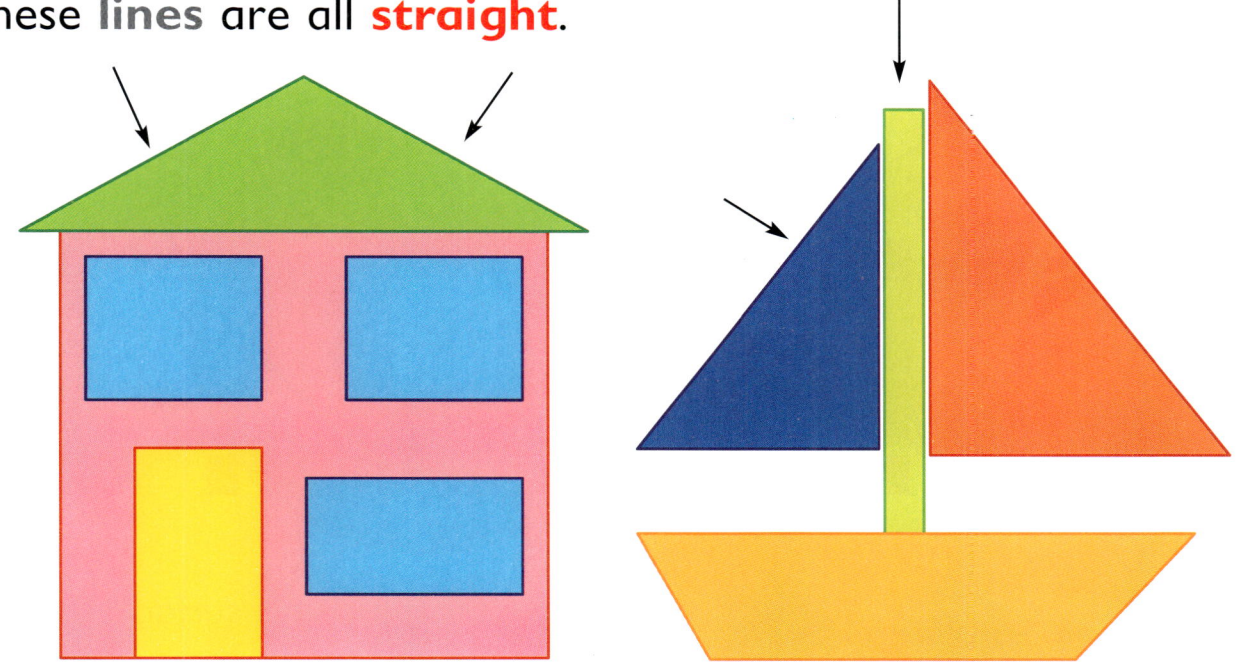

## subtract, subtraction   See also: operation

We **subtract** when we take away and see how many are left.
Subtract means 'take away' or '**minus**'.

Five take away
two leaves three.

**5 – 2 = 3**

Six **minus** one leaves five.

**6 – 1 = 5**

These are **subtractions**.
Subtraction is the opposite of **addition**.

41

## surface

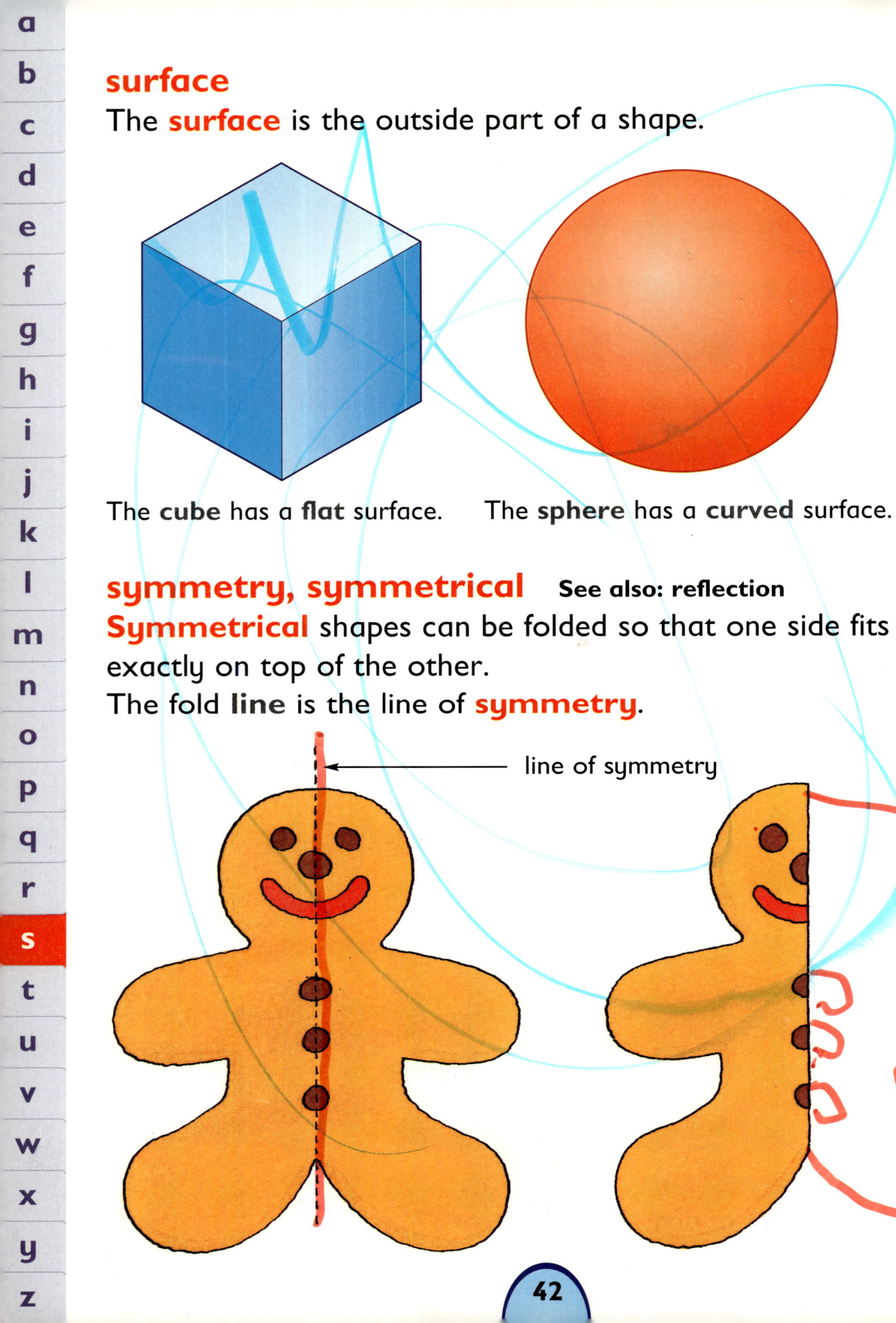

The **surface** is the outside part of a shape.

The **cube** has a **flat** surface.   The **sphere** has a **curved** surface.

## symmetry, symmetrical   See also: reflection

**Symmetrical** shapes can be folded so that one side fits exactly on top of the other.
The fold **line** is the line of **symmetry**.

← line of symmetry

## tall, taller, tallest

**Tall** is used to describe height.

The monsters are tall.

3 metres

The blue monster is 3 **metres** tall.
The red monster is **taller** than the blue monster.
The yellow monster is the **tallest**.

## tape measure

A **tape measure** helps you find out the **length** of objects.
It is marked with **centimetres** and **metres**.

## thousand

One **thousand** is the name for ten **hundreds**.

… 991 992 993 994 995 996 997 998 999 **1000**

## three-digit number

These are **three-digit numbers**.

**153**   **403**   **755**   **269**

They each have three **digits**: a **hundreds** digit, a tens digit and a **units** digit.

153 ⟶ 1 hundred, 5 tens and 3 units

## times table

These are **times tables**. The answers are **multiples**.

| | | |
|---|---|---|
| 1 x 2 = 2 | 1 x 5 = 5 | 1 x 10 = 10 |
| 2 x 2 = 4 | 2 x 5 = 10 | 2 x 10 = 20 |
| 3 x 2 = 6 | 3 x 5 = 15 | 3 x 10 = 30 |
| 4 x 2 = 8 | 4 x 5 = 20 | 4 x 10 = 40 |
| 5 x 2 = 10 | 5 x 5 = 25 | 5 x 10 = 50 |
| 6 x 2 = 12 | 6 x 5 = 30 | 6 x 10 = 60 |
| 7 x 2 = 14 | 7 x 5 = 35 | 7 x 10 = 70 |
| 8 x 2 = 16 | 8 x 5 = 40 | 8 x 10 = 80 |
| 9 x 2 = 18 | 9 x 5 = 45 | 9 x 10 = 90 |
| 10 x 2 = 20 | 10 x 5 = 50 | 10 x 10 = 100 |
| Times two table x 2 table | Times five table x 5 table | Times ten table x 10 table |

## tomorrow
**Tomorrow** is the day after today.
If today is Monday, tomorrow is Tuesday.

## total
The **total** is the answer to an **addition**.

**20p + 10p + 5p = 35p**

**4 + 3 = 7**

Total: 35p

Total: 7

## triangle, triangular
A **triangle** has 3 **straight sides** and 3 **corners**.

These signs are **triangular**.
They are triangle shaped.

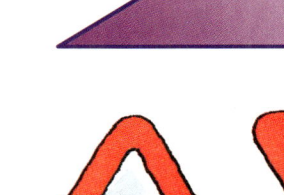

## twice
**See also: double**

**Twice** means two times.

The dog barks twice.

A six is thrown twice.

## two-digit number

These are **two-digit numbers**. They each have two **digits**: a tens digit and a units digit.

35 → 3 tens and 5 units

## unit

A **unit** is one thing or object. In a **number** the units **digit** tells how many ones or units there are.

48 → 4 tens and 8 units

## week
**See also: fortnight, weekend, year**

A **week** is 7 **days**.

Monday 8
Tuesday 9
Wednesday 10
Thursday 11
Friday 12
Saturday 13
Sunday 14

## weekend

The **weekend** is Saturday and Sunday.
You do not go to school on these **days**.

## weigh, weight

You **weigh** something to find out how **heavy** it is.
You are finding its **weight**.
A force called gravity gives you weight.

The tomatoes weigh 600 **grams**.

The cat weighs 4 **kilograms**.

## whole turn    See also: half turn, quarter turn

A **whole turn** goes all the way round, and comes back to where it started.

The rides make lots of whole turns.

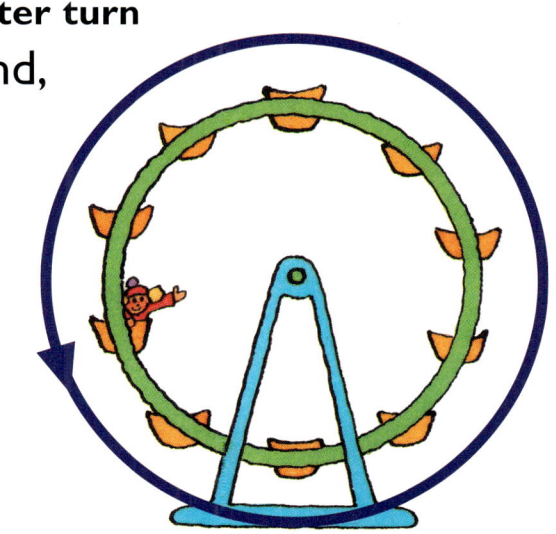

## year

A **year** is 12 **months**.
A year is 52 **weeks**.
A year is 365 **days**.
There are 4 **seasons** in a year.

Simon is 6 years old.

**BIRTHDAYS**

| January | February | March |
|---|---|---|
| Chloe Simon Lucy | Saif Emily | Paul Josh Holly |
| **April** | **May** | **June** |
| Mia Jack | Zoe Ravi Ellie | Sam Megan |
| **July** | **August** | **September** |
| Liam Amy | Alex Sarah | Sophie Mark Lena |
| **October** | **November** | **December** |
| Laura Tim | Luke Zoe | Jade Tom |

## yesterday

**Yesterday** was the **day** before today.
If today is Friday, yesterday was Thursday.

**WEATHER CHART**

| Monday | Tuesday | Wednesday | Thursday | Friday | Saturday | Sunday |
|---|---|---|---|---|---|---|
| ☀ | ☀ | ☁ | 🌧 | ☀ | | |

*It rained yesterday.*

## zero

**Zero** means **nought** or nothing.

It is written as **0**.